WHAT DO YOU Know!

TURNING POINTS OF WORLD WAR II

PEARL HARBOR, HIROSHIMA & NAGASAKI, D-DAY

Robin Johnson, Lynn Peppas, and Martha Martin

A Crabtree Canopy Book

Crabtree Publishing
crabtreebooks.com

Authors: Robin Johnson, Lynn Peppas, and Martha Martin
Editor: Kathy Middleton
Proofreader: Melissa Boyce
Design: Samara Parent
Production manager: Candice Campbell

IMAGE CREDITS

Library of Congress: p 4-5 (bkgd); p 9; p 11 (bottom); p 14-15, p 34, p 36-37

National Archives & Record Administration: Public Domain, p 11 (top)

Shutterstock: Charlesimage, p 6; Altrendo Images, p 12; adolf martinez soler, p 31 (bottom); JANDI, p 38 (top); Picture Partners, p 39; Sean Pavone p 40 (bottom)

US Navy: Public Domain, p 10

Wikimedia Commons: National Archives and Records Administration, p 5, p 13, p 22, p30, p 31 (top); public domain, pgs 8, 18, 19, 23, 25, 26, 28, 29, 32, 33, 35, 37 (top), 44, 45, 46, 47, 48, 50, 51, 52, 53, 54, 55, 56, 57, 58, 59 Time Life Pictures, p 24; German Federal Archives, p 42; Russian International News Agency (RIA Novosti), p 43 (bottom); Raymond Douglas Veydt, p 57 (top); UK in France, p 61 (bottom)

All other images from Shutterstock

Crabtree Publishing

crabtreebooks.com 800-387-7650

In Canada: We acknowledge the financial support of the Government of Canada through the Canada Book Fund for our publishing activities.

Printed in the U.S.A./CP2025

Published in Canada
Crabtree Publishing
616 Welland Ave.
St. Catharines, Ontario
L2M 5V6

Published in the United States
Crabtree Publishing
347 Fifth Ave.
Suite 1402-145
New York, NY 10016

Library and Archives Canada Cataloguing in Publication
Available at Library and Archives Canada

Library of Congress Cataloging-in-Publication Data
Available at the Library of Congress

Hardcover: 978-1-0398-9768-7
Ebook (pdf): 978-1-0398-8180-8
Epub: 978-1-0398-8300-0

CONTENTS

Chapter 1 – Pearl Harbor

The Road to War 4

Plan of Attack 8

Surprise Attack 10

Picking up the Pieces 15

This Means War! 18

Remember Pearl Harbor 20

Chapter 2 – Hiroshima & Nagasaki

Nuclear Nightmare 22

The World at War 25

Atomic Attack 31

Death and Destruction 36

Rising from the Ashes 40

Chapter 3 – D-Day

Preparing for D-Day 42

D-Day Begins.. 48

Operation Neptune.. 51

After D-Day 60

Glossary.. 62

Learning More.. 63

Index 64

CHAPTER 1

PEARL HARBOR

The attack on Pearl Harbor came as a complete surprise. Men scrambled to escape as the battleships went up in smoke.

The Road to War

On December 7, 1941, sailors in the U.S. Navy at Pearl Harbor woke to a terrible shock. The sky was swarming with aircraft marked with the Rising Sun. Bombs were raining down and exploding all around them. The United States was under attack by Japan!

Japan destroyed a dozen U.S. warships and killed more than 2,400 men that day. Although World War II had been raging in Europe for two years, the surprise strike shocked Americans—and the rest of the world. Striking back, the United States declared war on Japan the next day and joined the fighting in World War II.

During the Great Depression, people waited in long lines for free food. They could not afford to buy the fine items that were shipped from Japan.

Tension had been building between Japan and the United States for many years. The trouble started during the Great Depression. The Great Depression was a period when the worldwide **economy** was very poor. It began in 1929 and lasted for ten years. During that time, a lot of businesses failed and many people did not have jobs.

Japan was hit hard by the Great Depression. It was an island nation with only a few natural resources. Its economy relied on trading goods with other countries. However, the United States wanted Americans to buy products made in America to boost its own economy. In 1930, the U.S. government raised the taxes it charged other countries to ship goods into the United States. That way, fewer products from other countries could compete with American-made products. Other countries soon raised their fees too.

Japan needed resources to fuel its factories and make goods. It imported oil, coal, iron, steel, and rubber from other countries. Japan exported silk and other fine goods to places around the world.

Attacking for Oil

Japan had many factories, but it needed oil and other resources to run them. When trading costs rose, Japan could not afford to buy the resources it needed. So Japan's emperor, Hirohito, decided to grow Japan's **empire** instead. The Japanese began invading nearby countries to get their resources.

In 1931, Japan conquered a part of China called Manchuria. Six years later, the Japanese began storming the rest of China and taking it by force. In 1941, they invaded countries in Southeast Asia, including Cambodia, Laos, and Vietnam. Japan needed resources—and would do whatever it took to get them.

Hirohito became Emperor of Japan in 1926. He was determined to improve Japan's economy, even if it meant war.

> *"One man's life or death is a matter of no importance. All that matters is the Empire."*
>
> *Admiral Isoroku Yamamoto, the leader of Japan's navy*

U.S. president Franklin D. Roosevelt did not agree with Japan's attacks on Southeast Asia. He stopped American trade with Japan in July 1941. At the time, Japan got most of its oil and other resources from the United States. With the **embargo** in place, Japan could not grow its economy, its army, or its empire.

The U.S. Navy sent ships to keep the peace in Southeast Asia. The Japanese believed that if U.S. ships no longer patrolled the Pacific Ocean between Japan and the United States, Japan could invade other countries and get the oil it needed. To stop the patrols, Japan decided to destroy the U.S. **fleet** at Pearl Harbor.

World War II began in Europe on September 1, 1939, when Germany invaded Poland. Soon Britain, France, and many other countries were at war. In 1941, the world was watching the fighting in Europe. No one noticed Japan preparing to attack the United States.

This map shows the position of Pearl Harbor in Hawaii in relation to Japan.

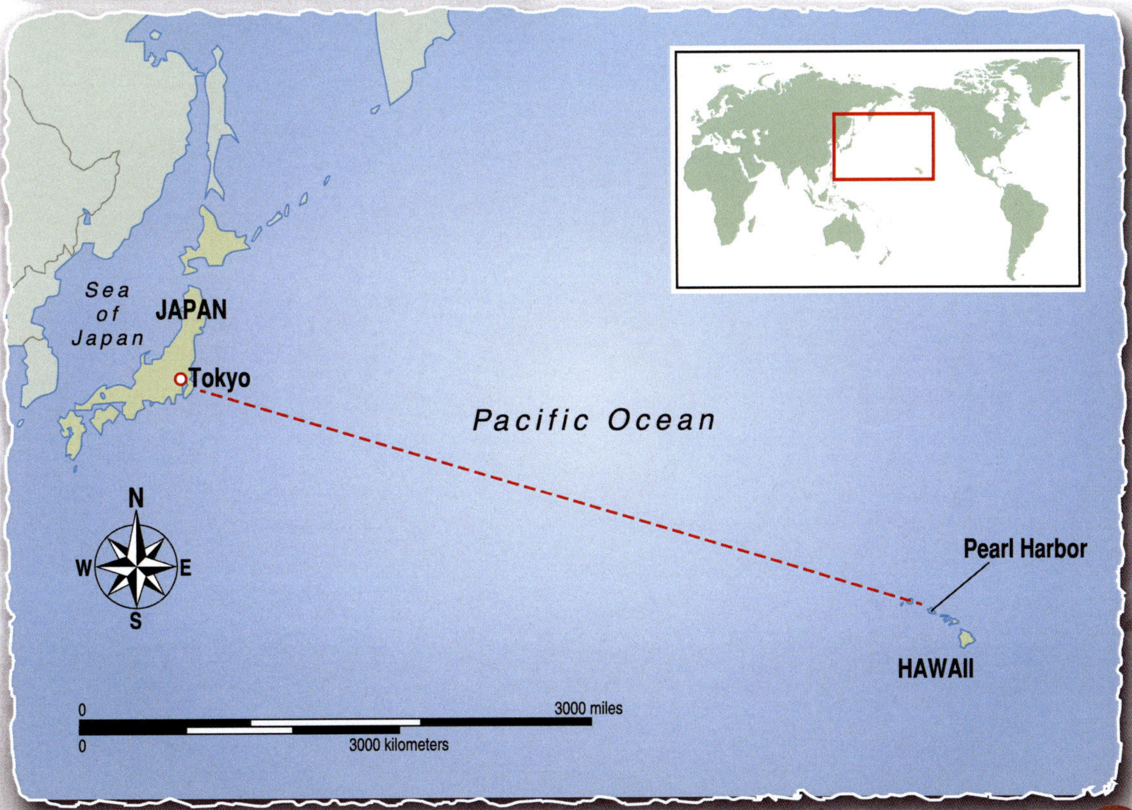

Japanese airmen trained to hit precise targets in their fast, low-flying planes.

Plan of Attack

Admiral Isoroku Yamamoto was in charge of Japan's navy. He began planning a daring **air raid** on Pearl Harbor in early 1941. His goal was to take the Pacific fleet out of action for at least six months. Yamamoto knew that the Japanese had to hit Pearl Harbor with a quick and crushing blow, or their risky plan would fail. Surprise was a key part of the attack. The United States must not see them coming.

Admiral Yamamoto spent many months preparing his men for the air raid. He sent spies to Pearl Harbor to gather information about the target. He built models of the harbor and American warships and studied them with his men. Yamamoto ran drills in a shallow harbor in Japan that was similar to Pearl Harbor. At last, Japan was ready to strike.

Isoroku Yamamoto had studied and worked in the United States. He knew that Americans would not give up without a fight. Yamamoto also realized that Japan was no match for the United States. Japan had a strong, well-trained army, but America was bigger and had many more resources.

In mid-November, a fleet of Japanese submarines headed for Hawaii. Five of the subs carried small underwater craft called midget submarines. Midget subs held two men and two torpedoes. They were used to invade harbors and other small spaces. Japan would use the mini subs to sneak into Pearl Harbor and **ambush** the Americans by sea.

On November 26, a fleet of more than 30 warships left Japan. Six massive ships, called aircraft carriers, transported hundreds of torpedo planes, bombers, and fighter planes. The planes took off from the ships and ambushed the Americans by air. The large Japanese fleet of ships dropped anchor about 274 miles (440 km) from Pearl Harbor.

Midget submarines like this were an important part of Japan's surprise attack plan.

About an hour before the air strike, an American destroyer called the USS *Ward* spied a midget submarine near Pearl Harbor. The Americans fired the first shots and sank the sub. The naval base at Pearl Harbor did not find out about the enemy submarine until the air raid was already underway.

Surprise Attack

December 7, 1941, began like any normal Sunday at the Pearl Harbor naval base. The sailors ate breakfast in mess halls. Some prepared to raise the flag, while others got ready for church. Many men were still sleeping when their nightmare began at Pearl Harbor.

Around 7:55 a.m., Americans noticed planes flying in the distance. At first, they figured it was just a training drill. After all, the United States was not at war and had not been alerted to danger. As the planes got closer, they saw the Rising Sun on the sides of the planes. They knew then it was not a drill.

This picture shows Pearl Harbor just before the attack. The Japanese planned the assault for Sunday morning because they knew American sailors would be relaxing then.

Suddenly, the sky above Pearl Harbor was filled with Japanese aircraft! Dive bombers dipped low over the ships docked in the harbor. They began dropping bombs on the unsuspecting crews below. The sky flashed and shouts rang out as the first bombs smashed into the ships.

The bombs woke the sleeping sailors in a hurry! They scrambled to get dressed and get to their posts. But the men were not prepared for battle. Their **ammunition** was locked up. Their ships were packed closely together in plain sight. The men were trapped in the harbor with no escape.

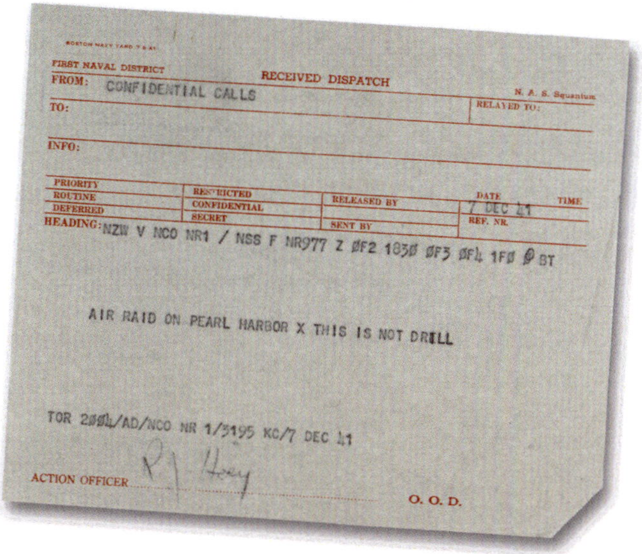

FIRST NAVAL DISTRICT
RECEIVED DISPATCH
FROM: CONFIDENTIAL CALLS
N. A. S. Squantum
TO:
RELAYED TO:
INFO:
PRIORITY
ROUTINE
DEFERRED
RESTRICTED
CONFIDENTIAL
SECRET
RELEASED BY
SENT BY
DATE 7 DEC 41
TIME
REF. NR.
HEADING: NZW V NCO NR1 / NSS F NR977 Z ØF2 1830 ØF3 ØF4 1FØ Ø BT

AIR RAID ON PEARL HARBOR X THIS IS NOT DRILL

TOR 20ØØ/AD/NCO NR 1/5195 KC/7 DEC 41
ACTION OFFICER
O. O. D.

Admiral Husband Kimmel at Pearl Harbor sent an urgent message to the U.S. Navy fleet at 8:00 a.m.

This photograph was taken by a Japanese pilot as he approached Pearl Harbor.

First Strike

Japanese planes targeted the American battleships first. Battleships were huge, powerful warships filled with people and weapons. Japan **bombarded** the battleships with underwater missiles dropped from torpedo planes. They also used fighter planes to destroy American aircraft before they could take off.

Despite their shock, American sailors acted quickly. About five minutes into the attack, they began to fight back. Several American gunners reached their posts. They loaded anti-aircraft guns and tried to shoot down the Japanese planes. A handful of American fighter pilots reached their planes and took to the air. They shot down a few enemy aircraft but were greatly outnumbered by the Japanese.

> *"Smoke was spreading rapidly over the harbor. Very shortly the day became black as night; it was terrifying beyond means of description."*
>
> *George Macartney Hunter, an officer on the USS* West Virginia

The names of the men who went down with the USS Arizona are carved on a memorial at Pearl Harbor.

At 8:10 a.m., a battleship called the USS *Arizona* was hit hard. A heavy bomb slammed through the ship's deck and into its **magazine**. More than a million pounds (450,000 kg) of explosives had been stored there. The ship burst into a giant ball of flames.

Less than 10 minutes after it was hit, the mighty ship had sunk, with much of its crew still on board. Nearly 1,200 officers and crewmen were killed on the USS *Arizona* that day. It was the greatest loss of life on any warship in the history of the U.S. Navy.

Thick black clouds filled the air as the USS Arizona went up in smoke.

Another battleship called the USS *Oklahoma* was hit by torpedoes early in the attack. Some men abandoned the ship as it was starting to roll over. But they did not give up the fight. Braving gunfire from low-flying planes, the men climbed onto the nearby USS *Maryland* and continued to defend the harbor.

Just 12 minutes after it was hit, the USS *Oklahoma* capsized, or tipped over. Many men were trapped inside the huge battleship. Rescuers cut holes in the ship and tried to pull the men to safety. Some sailors were saved, but many were not. They went down with their ship in Pearl Harbor that day.

Second Strike

There was a break in the bombing around 8:40 a.m. Then Japanese aircraft came back to finish what they had started. Some planes bombarded the battleships that were already in trouble. They pounded them with torpedoes again and again. Others targeted cruisers, destroyers, and other warships that had not been destroyed in the first wave of the attack.

Japanese dive bombers targeted a battleship that was trying to get away. The USS *Nevada* had raised anchor and was steaming out to sea. It was hit by a torpedo and several bombs along the way, however. The Americans were forced to **beach** their own ship so it would not sink and block the exit out of the harbor for other ships.

A total of 353 Japanese aircraft attacked Pearl Harbor that day, including 78 Mitsubishi A6M Zero planes. The Japanese Zero was a fast, lightweight fighter plane—and the terror of the Pacific. It could travel far from its carrier, make steep climbs and drops, dart around other aircraft, and hit targets from great distances.

These sailors are decorating the graves of men who died during the attack on Pearl Harbor.

Picking up the Pieces

By 9:45 a.m., Japanese bombers had left Pearl Harbor. The entire attack lasted less than two hours and left 2,403 Americans dead. Most were sailors who were on the ships when the bombs hit. Soldiers, airmen, marines, and **civilians** were also killed in the deadly air raid.

Some men survived the brutal attack but were seriously injured. Nearly 1,200 men were wounded in battle that day. Many were badly burned in the fiery blasts. Others had lost arms or legs when the bombs exploded. None of the survivors would ever be the same.

"It was just terrible. It was one of those things when you think, what's the world coming to?"

Horace Warden, Medical Officer on the USS Breese

The Damage

The U.S. Navy fleet was crushed at Pearl Harbor. A dozen ships were sunk or beached, including five huge battleships. Three battleships, three cruisers, three destroyers, and a number of other ships were damaged in the air raid. Nearly 200 American planes were also destroyed.

Luckily for the United States, there were no American aircraft carriers in the harbor that day. All three ships were out at sea. Important buildings—such as the power station and oil storage tanks—were also not hit in the attack. The United States would need its ships and supplies to strike back at Japan.

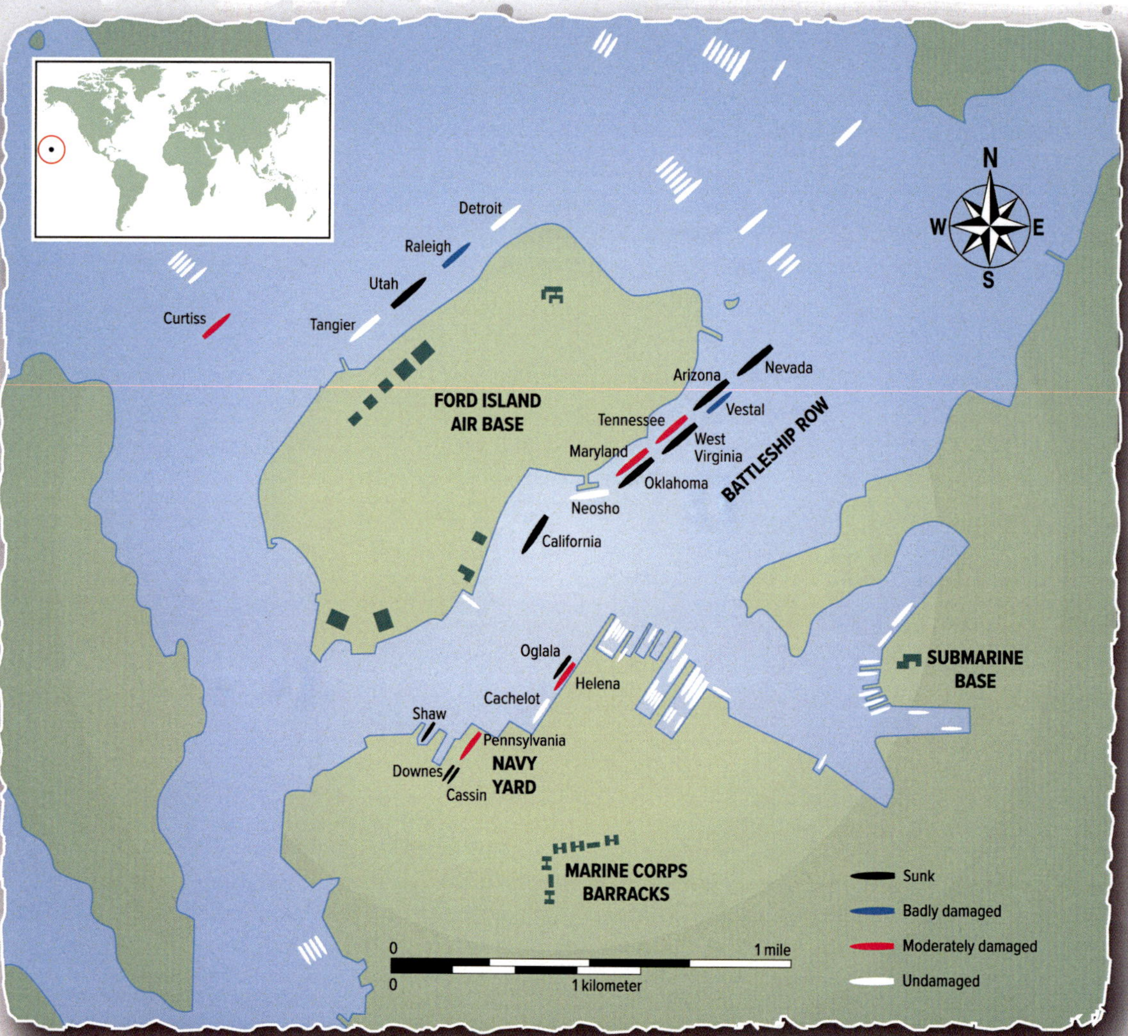

This map shows where the U.S. fleet was in Pearl Harbor that day, and how much damage was done. Battleships were large, armed warships, cruisers were smaller battleships, and destroyers were fast ships used to protect the fleet.

Other Targets

Pearl Harbor was not Japan's only target on December 7, 1941. Japanese forces also attacked several other islands in the western Pacific Ocean. They hit the U.S. territories of Guam, the Philippines, Wake Island, and Midway Island. They also attacked the British **colonies** of Hong Kong and Malaya.

Japan planned to take over the islands and get control of their resources before the United States and Britain could strike back. Japanese planes dropped bombs on the islands. Then ground **troops** landed and captured the islands—all except one. Midway Island held off the Japanese troops and won the first American victory of World War II.

The Rising Sun symbol was used on Japanese flags—and warplanes—until the end of World War II.

In 1941, Hawaii was a territory of the United States. A territory is a part of a country that does not have full rights as a state. Hawaii became the 50th state of the United States on August 21, 1959.

This Means War!

Japan had hoped that the attack on Pearl Harbor would break the Americans. Instead, it brought them roaring into World War II. Before the attack, the United States was fiercely divided. Some people were eager to fight in Europe, while others did not want to join a faraway war they felt did not concern them. The attack on Pearl Harbor brought Americans together with a shared goal—to get revenge on Japan.

On December 8, President Roosevelt gave an important speech to the U.S. Congress, the only part of the government with the power to declare war on another country. Roosevelt called the day Pearl Harbor was attacked "a date which will live in **infamy**." He also said that Americans were "in grave danger" and urged Congress to take action. Later that day, the United States declared war on the Empire of Japan. Britain also declared war on Japan that day for attacks against its colonies.

On December 11, Germany and Italy declared war on the United States. The two countries were **allies** of Japan during World War II. These declarations of war drew Americans into the fight in Europe too. The United States had no choice but to enter World War II and join forces with Great Britain and its allies to defeat Germany.

Posters called for Americans to do their duty and avenge those who died at Pearl Harbor.

"I fear that all we have done is awaken a sleeping giant."

Japanese Admiral Isoroku Yamamoto, who had warned what might happen if Japan provoked the United States into declaring war

American troops fought on land and at sea. The final blow to Japan came in August 1945. A new and extraordinarily powerful weapon called the atomic bomb was used for the first and only time in history. The United States dropped atomic bombs on the Japanese cities of Hiroshima and Nagasaki. The cities were almost completely wiped out, and more than 100,000 people were killed. On September 2, 1945, Japan surrendered. With Germany's surrender a few months earlier, World War II was finally over.

War at Home

In the United States, the war had created hardship for Americans of Japanese heritage. After Pearl Harbor was attacked, many Americans did not trust Japanese people living in the United States. Americans feared the Japanese were spying on them or would try to hurt them. So President Roosevelt had Japanese Americans sent to guarded **internment** camps.

More than 110,000 Japanese, including children, were shipped to these War Relocation Centers. Called "enemy aliens," some were immigrants from Japan, but nearly two-thirds of the prisoners were American citizens. Some families took a few belongings with them, but many had only the clothes on their backs. For the rest of the war, they were forced to live in dirty, crowded buildings with little food to eat.

U.S. Marines land supplies on the Japanese island of Iwo Jima after it had been captured in a fierce battle.

Remember Pearl Harbor

More than 80 years after the attack on Pearl Harbor and after 10 official investigations, people still have questions about that day of infamy. Why was America not ready for the attack? Were there clues that the Japanese were coming? Did the air raid on Pearl Harbor help or hurt Japan in the end?

Some people suspected that Japan might be planning to attack the United States. In February 1941, U.S. Admiral Richmond Turner warned that a "surprise attack upon the Fleet or Naval Base at Pearl Harbor" by Japan was "easily possible." Turner asked for Pearl Harbor to be put on high alert—but it was not.

There were also warning signs much closer to the day of the attack. In early December, the United States cracked some coded messages from Japan. The Americans learned that Japan was planning a major Pacific strike. They did not know where or when the attack would take place, however. Most people believed that Japan would target the Philippines or Malaya—not Hawaii.

About an hour before the attack, the American **radar** station in Oahu spotted a large group of planes heading to Hawaii from the north. A radar operator alerted the officer in charge right away. The equipment and the officer were both new to the job, and although he reported it, he was told the planes were American B-17 bombers. It was a grave mistake.

A deadly error was made when the Japanese planes approaching Pearl Harbor were mistaken for American planes.

The Arizona Memorial

"Remember Pearl Harbor!" became a battle cry that pushed American troops to carry on during World War II. Today, people visit Pearl Harbor to remember the **victims** who died there. More than a million tourists visit the USS *Arizona* Memorial in Hawaii each year.

The USS *Arizona* was filled with oil when it sank in Pearl Harbor so long ago. Today, drops of the oil still bubble up from the wreck every day, closely monitored by the National Park Service. People call the drops the "tears of the *Arizona*." In 1999, the USS *Missouri*—the battleship on which the Japanese officially surrendered—was moored next to the *Arizona* at Pearl Harbor.

In 1988, an Act of Congress was passed that said the United States had been wrong to imprison Japanese Americans after the attack. It gave compensation to the families. In 1991, President George W. Bush issued a formal apology for the government's actions at that time.

Americans wore buttons like this during the war, to remember what their country was fighting for.

Many visitors pay their respects at the USS Arizona Memorial in Pearl Harbor, where the sunken ship can be seen in the water.

CHAPTER 2

HIROSHIMA & NAGASAKI

Nuclear Nightmare

Monday, August 6, 1945, began like most other days for the 255,000 citizens of Hiroshima, Japan. Around 7 a.m., an air-raid alarm sounded. The people of Hiroshima were used to hearing it. Enemy aircraft often flew over the city, but they rarely dropped bombs.

An hour later, the all-clear signal sounded, telling the people of Hiroshima they could safely go about their lives. By 8:14 a.m., people were on their way to work. Children were playing outside or getting ready for school. All that changed in a split second when an atomic bomb was dropped on the city. This weapon was more destructive than any other in history.

The atomic bomb's mushroom-shaped cloud rose more than 9 miles (14.5 km) above the city of Hiroshima.

The atomic bomb—also called a **nuclear** bomb or an A-bomb—was a brand new weapon. It had never been used in a place where large numbers of people lived. It had only been tested in areas where no one lived. When the bomb dropped, it destroyed almost everything within 3 miles (5 km) of ground zero, or the point where it hit.

This map shows the Japanese cities of Hiroshima and Nagasaki, where the atomic bombs were dropped in August 1945.

The Atomic Bomb

An atomic bomb gets its energy when atoms of heavy metals such as uranium or plutonium are broken or split apart. The splitting of atoms is called fission. In an atomic bomb, fission takes place in one of two ways. Either a bullet of uranium is shot at more uranium (or plutonium) to split the atoms, or the atoms are forced together so violently by an explosive substance that they split apart.

The second atomic bomb, dropped on Nagasaki, was called Fat Man. It was powered by plutonium.

The Age of Nuclear Science

Throughout the 1930s, scientists studied nuclear physics—the science of the tiny particles in atoms—in great detail. But it was not until 1938 that a group of German scientists discovered nuclear fission. The best scientists from around the world knew that if they could build a bomb using this science, it would be a hugely powerful weapon. The race was on to create the first atomic bomb.

In August 1939, U.S. president Franklin Roosevelt received a letter from the famous scientist Albert Einstein. In the letter, he described the dreadful potential of an atomic bomb. He also explained that German scientists were already working on such a weapon. Roosevelt decided that the United States must build the bomb before Germany did.

Hungarian-born scientist Leo Szilard (right) wrote the letter to send to President Roosevelt. He asked Einstein (left) to sign it because Einstein was world famous and greatly respected.

> *"A single bomb of this type carried by boat and exploded in a* ***port*** *might very well destroy the whole port together with some of the surrounding territory."*
>
> *Albert Einstein, in his letter to President Roosevelt*

The World at War

In the 1930s, there was unrest in Europe. The German leader Adolf Hitler wanted to make Germany powerful by taking over other countries. When he invaded Poland in 1939, World War II broke out. Britain, France, Canada, and Russia, known as the Allies, fought against Germany, Japan, and Italy, known as the Axis powers.

The United States did not join the war right away. But President Roosevelt kept a careful eye on events in Europe. He was also worried about how much power Japan had. Japan had invaded China, so the United States and other countries placed an oil embargo on Japan. Without oil, the Japanese army could not fight for long.

World War II is the deadliest war ever fought in terms of numbers killed. More than 50 million people died during the six years that the war lasted. Half of these were soldiers, but the rest were regular citizens.

Adolf Hitler watches German soldiers march through the streets of Poland's capital, Warsaw, after the invasion that triggered World War II.

Leading to War

For the first two years of the war, the United States remained **neutral**. But the U.S. government helped the Allies by sending them supplies. The Japanese worried that the United States might send troops to stop them from fighting in Asia. To prevent this, Japan planned a secret attack on the United States.

On the morning of December 7, 1941, Japan attacked the U.S. naval base at Pearl Harbor in Hawaii. The assault took everyone by surprise. American fighter pilots scrambled to their planes to fight back in the skies. But the damage had already been done. Four battleships were sunk and almost 200 aircraft destroyed. Thousands of soldiers were killed.

The United States was now drawn into World War II. More than ever, Roosevelt realized the importance of having the most advanced weapons. He and other Allied leaders knew they had to create the atomic bomb first. If German scientists beat them to it, Germany would probably win the war.

Some of the world's greatest scientists came together to work on the Allied effort to build the atomic bomb. One of the project's leaders was the American J. Robert Oppenheimer (on the right).

The Manhattan Project

In September 1942, scientists from Britain, the United States, and Canada started working together to build the bomb. This was a top-secret project. Hardly anyone knew about it. One of the many places the scientists worked was in New York City, in the **borough** of Manhattan. The operation became known as the Manhattan Project.

The first large-scale nuclear reactor was built as part of the Manhattan Project in 1943. It still stands today.

The United States ended up spending over $2 billion on the Manhattan Project. Most of the money went toward building top-secret plants and producing materials to build the A-bomb.

A New President

President Roosevelt died suddenly on April 12, 1945, months before the first atomic bomb was even tested. The vice president, Harry Truman, became president. It was not an easy job to step into suddenly, especially during wartime. The Manhattan Project was so top secret that even Truman did not know about it until he became president.

> *"I felt like the moon, the stars, and all the planets had fallen on me."*
>
> *President Harry Truman, on becoming president*

World War II was a stormy time in history. Americans at home were dealing with shortages in food and supplies because of the war. Finally, on May 8, 1945, the weakened German army surrendered, ending World War II in Europe. But the conflict between the United States and Japan continued.

These American soldiers are attacking the Japanese island of Iwo Jima. The war in the Pacific region continued after the war in Europe ended.

The Trinity Test

By mid-July, the Manhattan Project scientists had built a bomb they called "Gadget." They prepared a special site to test it in a remote part of the desert in New Mexico, near Alamogordo. Gadget was lifted to the top of a 100-foot (30 m) steel tower ready for action. The code name for this atomic bomb test was "Trinity."

Around 5:30 a.m. on Monday, July 16, 1945, the first-ever atomic bomb explosion occurred. The steel tower **evaporated** instantly, and the explosion created a 1200-foot (366 m) crater. The heat from the bomb melted the desert sand, turning it into green glass. The explosion was more destructive than any of the scientists could have imagined. The Allies had won the race–they had an atomic weapon.

"The heat was like opening up an oven door, even at 10 miles."

A military policeman at base camp 10 miles (16 km) from the test site

Citizens of New Mexico saw and heard the atomic blast over 100 miles (160 km) away. To explain the huge explosion, army officials released a statement saying that a building filled with ammunition had blown up.

The Potsdam Meeting

The same month as the first atomic bomb test took place, Allied leaders met in the city of Potsdam in Germany. The war in Europe was over. Now the victors had to decide how to deal with the defeated nations. They also discussed what to do about Japan, which was still fighting the Allies.

Truman and the other leaders drew up a document known as the Potsdam Declaration. It called on Japan to surrender and end the war for good. If Japan refused, the Allies threatened to destroy Japan. The declaration was delivered to the Japanese on July 26, 1945. The Japanese government rejected the offer. Its army was determined to keep fighting.

"We call upon the government of Japan to proclaim now the unconditional surrender of all Japanese armed forces...the alternative for Japan is prompt and utter destruction."

The Potsdam Declaration

Allied leaders at the Potsdam Conference included President Harry Truman of the United States, Clement Attlee of Britain, and Joseph Stalin of the Soviet Union.

Atomic Attack

President Truman had a difficult decision to make. Should they use the atomic bomb? If the war continued, tens of thousands of American soldiers would probably be killed. If he dropped an atomic bomb on Japan, tens of thousands of Japanese civilians could be killed. Truman decided that to end the war as soon as possible, the atomic bomb must be used against Japan. He gave the order.

"Little Boy" was the code name for the first-ever atomic bomb to be used during wartime. It was called this because it was thinner than other atomic bombs. Little Boy was boarded on a B-29 U.S. Air Force bomber called *Enola Gay*.

U.S. president Harry Truman was left with the terrible job of deciding whether or not to use an atomic bomb during World War II.

Little Boy was hardly little! It weighed 9,700 pounds (4,400 kg), stood over 10 feet (3 m) tall, and had a diameter of 28 inches (71 cm).

The uranium-powered atomic bomb named Little Boy had the explosive power of about 200,000 regular bombs used during World War II.

Target: Hiroshima

The *Enola Gay* was piloted by Colonel Paul Tibbets Jr., with another 11 crew members on board. The plane took off from a U.S. air base about 1,400 miles (2,250 km) away from Japan at 2 a.m. on Monday, August 6, 1945. Its target was the Japanese city of Hiroshima.

Hiroshima was chosen because it was an industrial city. It had not been heavily bombed before and had little damage. Experts felt that they would be able to see the full effects of the A-bomb more clearly there. A timing device and change in air pressure would **activate** the bomb after it was released. Little Boy fell for 45 seconds before exploding about 1,900 feet (580 m) above Hiroshima.

"I knew we did the right thing...I thought, yes, we're going to kill a lot of people, but by God we're going to save a lot of lives."

Colonel Paul Tibbets Jr., pilot of the Enola Gay

When they boarded the plane, only Tibbets (in the center here) and two other crew members knew about Little Boy. Tibbets told the others what they were carrying on their way to Hiroshima.

The bomb exploded with a blinding flash of light. Almost immediately, a huge ball of fire began to spread over 3 miles (5 km). The temperature where the bomb struck was over 5,400 °Fahrenheit (3,000 °C). Everything within 1 mile (1.6 km) of the impact was vaporized instantly—humans, animals, plants, and buildings all vanished.

At the time of the atomic explosion, a powerful blast of air called a shock wave pushed outward. Strong winds traveled 7 miles (11 km) in 30 seconds. Windows and doors were blown out, and even entire buildings were destroyed. Winds carrying dirt and burned waste were sucked up into a giant fireball.

> *"The houses at the edge of the city...have collapsed or burned down.... Where the city stood, there is a gigantic burned-out scar."*
>
> *John Siemes, a priest*

Strong winds spread ***firestorms*** *that burned trees and buildings for over 25 miles (40 km) from ground zero.*

As the Japanese people tried to understand what had just happened in Hiroshima, the U.S. government issued a warning. If Japan did not surrender, the United States would drop another A-bomb. American aircraft dropped leaflets on cities in Japan, warning citizens of another attack. The Japanese government still refused to give in.

Fat Man and Nagasaki

Three days later, on August 9, 1945, a plutonium-powered A-bomb, code named "Fat Man," was dropped on the city of Nagasaki. Nagasaki had a thriving industry building ships for the Japanese navy. Fat Man was bigger and more powerful than Little Boy. It exploded about 1,800 feet (550 m) above Nagasaki and its population of 260,000.

The mountains surrounding Nagasaki helped to limit the destructive effects of the atomic explosion.

> *"My crew and I had flown to Nagasaki to end the war, not to inflict suffering."*
>
> *Charles Sweeney, the pilot of the plane that dropped the bomb on Nagasaki*

Japan Surrenders

Even after two atomic bomb attacks, some Japanese leaders still did not want to surrender. But Japan's emperor, Hirohito, did not want his people to suffer any more. At noon on August 15, he announced to the people of Japan that their country would surrender. The war was finally over.

On September 2, Japanese leaders signed an official document of surrender on board the U.S. Navy battleship USS *Missouri*. The day of Japan's surrender became known as Victory over Japan Day, or V-J Day. Since the end of the war, the anniversary of V-J Day is remembered on September 2 in the United States.

*"The [United States] has begun to employ a new and most cruel bomb, the power of which to do damage is, indeed, **incalculable**, taking the toll of many innocent lives."*

Emperor Hirohito, in his speech to the Japanese people on August 15, 1945

Japanese citizens adored their leader, Emperor Hirohito. Many believed he was a god.

Death and Destruction

The atomic bomb destroyed almost all the buildings at Nagasaki within 1 mile (1.6 km) of ground zero. All structures were burned or blown apart by the strength of the blast. There was even more destruction on the ground at Hiroshima. Almost all buildings within 3 miles (5 km) were completely destroyed.

Even after the initial explosions, the bombs continued to cause death and destruction. Nuclear fallout is **radioactive** particles that are created during an atomic explosion. These particles get mixed in the dust and ash created by the explosion. They can be carried for miles by the strong winds. They then fall back to Earth and poison all living things.

Radiation released from an atomic explosion is an invisible killer. It enters the cells of a person's body and can kill them days, weeks, months, or even years after the bombing.

The low, flat ground of Hiroshima meant that the destruction of the bomb easily spread out.

More than 90 percent of the buildings of Hiroshima were destroyed by the atomic bomb.

At Hiroshima, about 45,000 people died instantly from the intense heat of the explosion. Near the site of the main blast, all living things were burned or died right away. All that was left was ash. Others died after being caught inside burning or collapsing buildings. In Nagasaki, the explosion immediately killed about 22,000 people.

Radioactive particles from the bomb were pushed up into a cloud by the **afterwinds**. The cloud was carried, and cooled, by the winds. About half an hour after the bomb exploded, a black, sticky rain fell back to Earth. The black rain spread its harmful radioactive material to even more people.

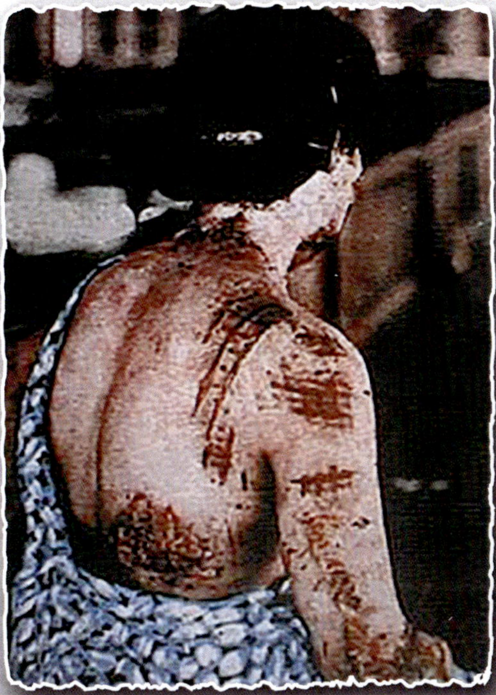

Those people who survived the blasts suffered terrible burns and radiation sickness.

Hiroshima survivors still bear the scars of the atomic bomb today.

Human Suffering

Thousands of people from Hiroshima and Nagasaki did not die instantly, but suffered from serious injuries. Some were burned by the radiation. Sometimes people's bones melted inside their bodies, causing them to become **disfigured**. Many died later from their injuries or from radiation poisoning.

The explosions killed many health care workers in both cities. They destroyed hospitals and emergency services. Thousands of people were seriously injured and needed medical attention. Many were trapped under fallen buildings—or inside burning buildings. But there were not enough people left to help those in need or to care for those who were suffering.

Overall, experts think that about 275,000 people died from the two atomic bombs. The people who survived the blasts in Hiroshima and Nagasaki are known as *hibakusha*, which means "people affected by the explosion."

People from Hiroshima and Nagasaki began to fall ill from radiation sickness just a few hours after the A-bombs exploded. Symptoms included hair loss, bleeding in the gums and under the skin, sores and swelling in the mouth and throat, nausea, fever, weight loss, and diarrhea. Within 10 days, people started dying from the radiation poisoning.

The horror did not end there. People developed cancers from the radiation years after the atomic bombs exploded. A young girl from Hiroshima named Sadako Sasaki was two years old when the atomic bomb was dropped. She survived the blast, but died 10 years later from a blood cancer called leukemia.

Sadako thought if she folded 1,000 paper cranes she might get better. Sadly, she died before she could finish. Today, children still put paper cranes on the peace memorial in Hiroshima.

Rising from the Ashes

After the war ended, the United States government put together a **reconstruction** plan. American soldiers and aid workers went to Japan to help rebuild cities such as Hiroshima and Nagasaki. The new cities were even better than before. The United States also worked to make Japan's economy and government better.

City planners wanted to rebuild Hiroshima as a city that symbolized peace. At ground zero, they built the Peace Memorial Park to honor the people who died because of the atomic bomb. The park covers about 25 acres (10 hectares) of land. It contains a museum, a Children's Peace Monument, and many other memorials.

The A-Bomb Dome was the only partially remaining building in Hiroshima after the bomb. It still stands today at Hiroshima's Peace Memorial Park.

Peace Memorial Park now stands where the bomb dropped on Hiroshima.

Every year on August 6, people gather at Peace Memorial Park. Some float colored paper lanterns in the Motoyasu River to remember those who died from the atomic bomb.

Life for the Hibakusha

Buildings were more easily rebuilt than the scars and injuries of the hibakusha. Many people faced **discrimination** after the bombings because of how they looked. A lot of them could not find work, and some were too hurt to be able to work. People did not want to marry survivors for fear their children would be born with birth defects.

In 1955, Kiyoshi Tanimoto and Norman Cousins began a project to help 25 women from Hiroshima who had been disfigured by the bomb blasts. The women were brought to New York City. Surgeons carried out 127 operations on these "Hiroshima Maidens" to improve the way they looked.

Nuclear Weapons Today

After World War II, other countries built atomic weapons, including Britain, France, and Russia. Although nuclear weapons have been tested by many nations, they have never been used again in war. It is estimated that there are about 12,000 nuclear weapons in the world today. Together, they have enough power to destroy all life on Earth.

The lives of Japanese survivors were changed forever when the atomic bomb was dropped. But the bombs also changed the lives of people around the world. The fact that such powerful weapons exist in the world frightens people. Some governments and campaigners are fighting to have all nuclear weapons destroyed.

In 1996, an agreement called the Comprehensive Test Ban Treaty was adopted by the United Nations. It was an agreement to end nuclear explosions in tests or in war. Some countries, including the United States, have still not **ratified** the treaty.

This statue of a woman with her child commemorates the women victims of the bomb that fell on Nagasaki.

CHAPTER 3

D-DAY

Adolf Hitler salutes his German soldiers as they march into Poland. This invasion started World War II.

Preparing for D-Day

On September 1, 1939, German troops invaded Poland. This was the start of World War II. The war lasted for six years. Fighting spread throughout the world. Germany, Japan, and Italy fought on the same side. They were called the "Axis powers." The German leader was Adolf Hitler.

Britain, Canada, the United States, and Russia fought against Hitler. These countries were called the Allies. The Allies had many soldiers and weapons, but so did Hitler. The two sides fought fierce battles. They were so evenly matched, no one could tell who would win the war.

Hitler was the leader of a German political party called the Nazi Party. His followers were called Nazis. The Nazis wanted Germany to be the strongest country in Europe.

"Fortress Europe"

Hitler's army invaded many countries in Europe. Hitler called these captured countries "**Fortress** Europe." He thought that if he controlled a lot of countries, he could defeat the Allies.

To the east of Germany, the Russians fought hard against the Germans. They stopped Hitler from taking over more land in the east. If the Allies could get into western Europe, they could squeeze Hitler's armies from both sides and take land back.

This map shows Europe in 1944. The dark green areas are countries that were controlled by Germany.

Early in the war, the Russian leader Joseph Stalin was on Hitler's side. But in 1941, Hitler invaded Russia too. After that, Russia changed sides and joined the Allies.

The Russian city of Stalingrad, in eastern Europe, was ***occupied*** *by the Germans. After months of fierce fighting and much destruction, Russian soldiers defeated the German army and won the city back.*

Operation Overlord

The Allies needed many soldiers and weapons to force the Germans out of the areas they had taken over. The Allies also needed a safe place to bring in men and supplies. France was the best choice. From there, the Allies could take back Europe. The only problem was that France was occupied by Germany.

The Allies came up with a daring plan to enter France. They called the plan "Operation Overlord." To begin the attack, the Allies would invade five beaches in France. They had to get the timing just right. The Allies would attack by both air and sea on a chosen day. They called that day "D-Day."

The "D" in "D-Day" does not stand for anything. D-Day is army code for the day of an attack. June 6, 1944, became the most famous "D-Day."

American General Eisenhower (third from right) discusses plans for D-Day with the British leader General Montgomery (right).

Hitler knew that the Allies were planning an invasion. He thought they would invade at the French town of Calais. It was closest to England. Hitler sent many German soldiers to Calais. But the Allies had used **double agents** to give Hitler the wrong information.

The Allies used other tricks too. In England, they set up fake boats and balloons that looked like tanks. They wired empty fields with lights. German pilots thought these were army camps. Even on D-Day, Hitler still thought Calais was the real target.

One of the most famous World War II double agents was Juan Pujol Garcia of Spain. His code name to the Allies was Garbo. To the Germans it was Arabal. He gave the Germans fake information about D-Day that made them believe it would take place at Calais.

Some pretend tanks could be blown up like balloons. Others were made of wood.

Eisenhower in Control

U.S. General Dwight Eisenhower was in charge of Operation Overlord. He knew the Allies needed more men and weapons for the attack to be successful. Eisenhower brought in another 1.6 million American troops. Thousands of tanks, planes, and weapons were taken to England each month.

The Allied troops trained hard. Soldiers practiced landing on beaches. **Paratroopers** practiced night landings. U.S. and British bomber planes prepared to bomb French roads and train tracks. This would make it hard for German soldiers to get through to stop the attack.

> *"We were all eager for action."*
>
> *Roland Johnson, Royal Canadian Artillery*

Tanks and guns were loaded onto boats in England in preparation for D-Day.

General Eisenhower wished the soldiers luck before they set off for France.

About 170,000 soldiers headed to the English coast. On May 31, 1944, they boarded thousands of **landing craft** and bigger ships. This was the first part of Operation Overlord. It would be the largest sea invasion ever. Its code name was "Operation Neptune."

Delay

The men were on the boats, ready to go. But they heard that bad storms were coming, so Eisenhower held off until June 5. Then he heard the weather would be better for the next 36 hours. D-Day was back on!

> *"The free men of the world are marching together to victory."*
>
> *General Dwight Eisenhower*

D-Day Begins

About 23,000 British and U.S. paratroopers took off from England. They were the first soldiers to land in France on D-Day. Their job was to capture important bridges and roads in the area. This would stop German **reinforcements** from getting to the beaches.

As the paratroopers jumped from the planes, Germans on the ground started shooting. Many paratroopers were killed. Others landed miles off course. Some paratroopers landed safely in the right place. They captured the bridges and roads. The invasion from the air was a success.

"Bullets were criss-crossing the sky. Many troopers were hit before landing."

*Joseph Beryl, U.S. Army Parachute **Infantry***

Paratroopers had to jump out of the planes carrying everything they would need to fight the Germans.

Russell, Steele, and Ray

U.S. paratroopers Ken Russell and John Steele were in trouble. Their plane had dropped them off target. Their parachutes got stuck on the church in the French town of Sainte-Mère-Église. The Germans could see them. They were trapped.

Another U.S. paratrooper, John Ray, had landed next to the church. A German soldier shot him. Then the German turned to shoot Russell and Steele. While he lay dying, Ray grabbed his gun. He killed the German before he could shoot again.

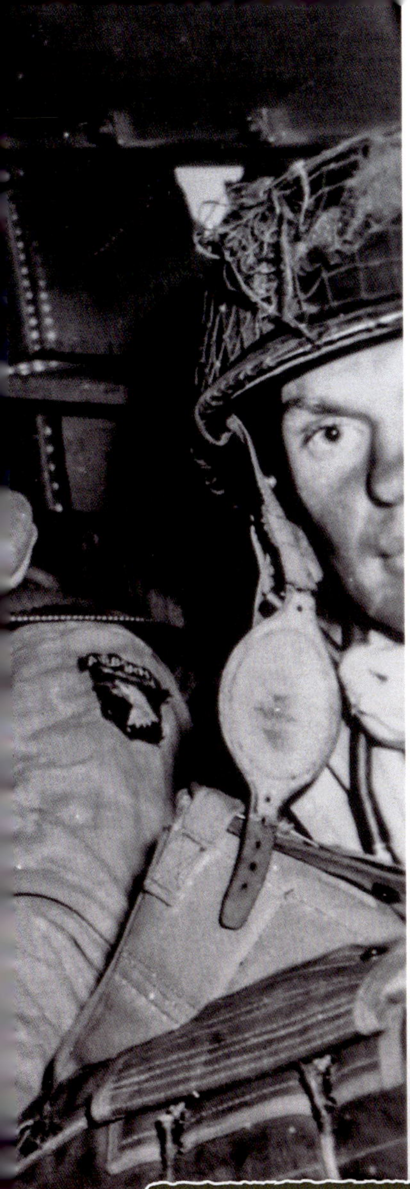

"We were all sitting ducks coming down."

Private Ken Russell, U.S. 82nd Airborne Division

To honor the brave U.S. paratroopers, a model of a paratrooper hangs from the church in Sainte-Mère-Église.

5:20 a.m.: Bomber Planes

Allied bombers flew in next. They needed to bomb German **defenses** on the shore so Allied troops could land safely. The weather was bad. The defenses were hard to see from the air. Many bombs missed their targets. Some planes returned to England without dropping any bombs at all.

These bomber planes are on a mission to France in May 1944. On D-Day, bombs were dropped from the air to destroy German guns near the beaches.

5:50 a.m.: Battleships

More bombing came from the sea. Allied battleships in the English Channel fired at the defenses on the shore. They did not hit enough targets. There were still thousands of German soldiers ready to fight back against the Allies.

"A steady rain was falling and we could hardly see.... But there was no holding back."

Allen W. Stephens, U.S. bomber pilot

Operation Neptune

Operation Neptune targeted five beaches for landings in **Normandy**. Each beach had a code name. The U.S. forces landed on "Utah" and "Omaha" to the west. The British had "Gold" in the middle and "Sword" to the east. The Canadians landed on "Juno," between Gold and Sword.

The Allies planned to use landing craft to get close to the shore. Tanks and weapons would be unloaded. Soldiers would wade through the water onto the beaches. These soldiers would try to destroy the German defenses. Then they would move inland to take back France.

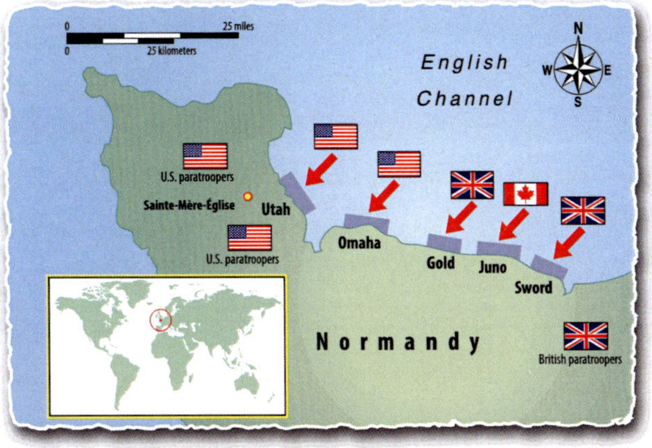

This map shows the five beaches where the Allies landed on June 6, 1944.

> *"Your task will not be an easy one."*
>
> *General Dwight Eisenhower*

Boats traveled together across the Channel for safety.

to be right. The tides were different on each beach. They could make the water too low or too high. Either one was bad.

The Americans landed first at Omaha and Utah. Then the British landed on Gold. The Canadians were next at Juno. The British forces at Sword were last. Operation Neptune was on!

The Germans put many "Czech hedgehogs" all along the shoreline. These defenses were made of crossed strips of metal. They destroyed many Allied boats.

U.S. soldiers had to wade through the water to the shore, under fire from the Germans.

“Bloody Omaha” Beach

Omaha Beach was heavily defended. The Germans put big guns on the high cliffs. They were ready when the U.S. infantry soldiers tried to land. Many never made it to shore. A lot of boats sank with their men inside. More than 3,000 American soldiers were killed or wounded at Omaha Beach.

The men who made it to shore fought hard. They were under constant fire. Slowly, some soldiers made it forward. A few climbed the cliffs in small groups. They destroyed the German guns. By afternoon, Omaha was in Allied hands.

“The bodies of the other guys washed ashore...my friends...in many cases, blown to pieces.”

Thomas Valence, U.S. 116th Infantry Rifle Sergeant

Utah Beach

Utah Beach was the closest to the port of Cherbourg in France. The Allies needed to capture Cherbourg so they could bring in supplies after D-Day. U.S. troops heading to Utah Beach in landing craft got pushed off course by the tides. They landed about 1 mile (1.6 km) off target.

This turned out to be lucky. The place where they actually landed was safer. The Allies lost only 300 men from the 20,000 that landed on Utah Beach. The mission was a success.

> *"We'll start the war from here!"*
>
> *General Theodore Roosevelt Jr., commander of the forces at Utah Beach*

Once on shore, the commander of Utah Beach decided to move inland from there instead of working their way back to the original target.

7:25 a.m.: Gold Beach

The British came close to Gold Beach, but the strong winds caused the tides to come in quickly. Now the water was too high. They could not see the German mines under the water. Many landing craft were damaged by mines.

British soldiers fought to reach shore. Germans shot at them from the beach. Luckily for the British, the biggest German guns had been destroyed by the bombings earlier in the day. By the end of the day, Gold Beach was also in Allied hands.

Once they had taken Gold Beach, the Allies built a "mulberry port." This was a temporary port so that they could unload cargo to supply the troops on the beaches.

The U.S. Coast Guard helped unload tanks and other vehicles during the attack on Gold Beach.

Stanley Hollis

British Sergeant Major Stanley Hollis landed on Gold Beach on D-Day. He was only 31, but he had fought in many battles. Hollis was already a hero to his men. On D-Day he became a hero again.

Stanley's men were under fire on Gold Beach. He saw some German gunners in a **pillbox**. Without any help, Stanley attacked the Germans and took them prisoner. Then he saw another pillbox. He captured the Germans in that one too!

Sword Beach

Sword was at the end of the five beaches. It was very important to the Allies. They had to capture and keep Sword Beach. If the Allies lost it, the Germans could reach the other beaches and take them back. This would mean that all the Allies' hard-won advances would be undone.

The Germans did not have very strong defenses at Sword Beach. British troops quickly took control of the beach, and then started moving inland. They were soon stopped by a group of powerful German tanks. This was the only armored **counterattack** that took place on D-Day, and the British won.

Within an hour of landing on Sword Beach, the British had fought their way inland.

Panzers vs. AVREs

The powerful German tanks near Sword Beach were called Panzers. The Allies knew they had to beat these big machines. They brought their own tanks across the Channel on D-Day. Some Allied tanks were designed especially for this operation.

AVRE stands for "Armoured Vehicle Royal Engineers." These were British tanks with some very useful features. They had **armor** at the front and escape hatches on each side. Many AVREs had huge guns called mortars. These saved a lot of Allied lives on D-Day.

Panzers were Germany's biggest and best tanks.

Major-General Percy Hobart designed many of the funny-looking tanks that the Allies used on D-Day. Today these tanks are known as "Hobart's Funnies."

AVREs were basic tanks that were adapted to include special features.

7:55 a.m.: Juno Beach

About 14,000 soldiers from Canada were sent to take Juno Beach. Many of their boats hit mines near the shore. One-third of the landing craft were sunk. Allied tanks were supposed to be on the beach first to protect the soldiers, but the tanks were late.

The Canadians pushed forward anyway. The men were under constant fire. More than 1,000 soldiers died on Juno Beach. Many more were hurt. **Medics** helped the wounded men. By the afternoon, the Allies controlled Juno Beach.

Wounded soldiers were taken by field ambulance to a protected area before being loaded onto a hospital ship.

The Canadian soldiers were given bicycles so they could carry more and travel faster.

This Canadian soldier is guarding Germans that have been captured on Juno Beach.

Charlie Martin

Charlie Martin was a farmer before World War II. During the war, he became a **Company** Sergeant Major. He was a brave soldier. After a battle, he would look for wounded men. He carried them to safety.

On D-Day, Martin led the first company of soldiers to land on Juno Beach. There were 250 men in Martin's company. More than half of them were killed. Martin and two of his men were able to capture a German machine gun. This saved many lives.

> *"I was so sad. Fellows I had known for four or five years ...destroyed for nothing."*
>
> *Charlie Martin*

After D-Day

The D-Day invasion was a success. The Allies took the beaches, but that was only the start. They used this base to bring in more men and supplies. They kept moving across France. By August 25, Paris, the capital of France, was free.

The war in Europe went on for 11 more months. Hitler killed himself on April 30, 1945. On May 7, Germany surrendered. Japan kept fighting until September 2, 1945. When Japan surrendered, World War II was finally over.

While the invasion of Normandy was a success, it caused heavy losses on both sides. By the time France was free, more than 200,000 Allies and 300,000 Germans had been killed, wounded, or captured.

The D-Day landings were a huge operation, involving thousands of men and machines.

D-Day Remembered

D-Day was a turning point in the war. It gave the Allies a way into Europe. It showed Hitler that he could be beaten. It gave hope to the people in the captured countries that they would be free again.

D-Day is still remembered today. Every year on June 6, people gather on the beaches of Normandy. More than 80 years later, most of the soldiers who served on D-Day have now died. The very few who are still alive are well over 90 years old.

This memorial statue on a beach at Normandy shows a soldier sheltering his wounded friend.

> *"These are the heroes who helped end a war."*
>
> *U.S. president Ronald Reagan, on the 40th anniversary of D-Day*

Displays such as this one on D-Day anniversaries are important reminders to everyone of the lives lost in defense of freedom.

GLOSSARY

activate To set off

afterwinds Strong winds caused by a bomb blast

air raid An attack by enemy planes

allies Countries who help each other in times of war

ambush To attack by surprise

ammunition Bullets and shells fired from weapons

armor Thick metal plates that provide protection

beach To run a ship onto shore

bombarded Attacked repeatedly with bombs

borough An area within a city with its own local government

civilians People who are not in the armed forces

colonies Places ruled by faraway leaders

company A group of soldiers that train and fight together

counterattack When an army attacks to win back lost ground

defenses Things used to protect something

discrimination Bad or unfair treatment

disfigured Changed from something's usual appearance

double agents Spies who work for two countries that are enemies

economy The money and resources in a country

embargo A government order to stop trading with a country

empire A large area of land that is ruled by one leader

evaporated Changed from a solid to a gas, effectively disappearing

firestorms Large, destructive fires fed by strong winds

fleet A group of warships that sail and work together

fortress A strong place that can be defended easily if it is attacked

incalculable So great that its cost cannot be measured

infamy Being famous for something bad

infantry Soldiers who fight on foot

internment Being held against one's will, especially in wartime

landing craft Flat-bottomed boats that can land on beaches

magazine A place where explosives are stored on a ship

medics Soldiers trained to be doctors on the battlefield

neutral Not involved in a conflict

Normandy A region of France

nuclear Powered by the energy released when atoms collide

occupied When one country has taken control of another country

paratroopers Soldiers who are trained to parachute into battle

pillbox A concrete shelter to protect soldiers when shooting

port A place where boats dock to load and unload goods

radar A device used to track planes and other moving objects

radioactive Giving off harmful rays when split by fission

ratified Formally approved and turned into a law

reconstruction Rebuilding

reinforcements New soldiers sent to help in a battle

tides The rise and fall of the ocean

troops Groups of soldiers

victims People who are hurt or killed in an attack

LEARNING MORE

Books

Boutland, Craig. *What Happened at Pearl Harbor?* Rosen Young Adult, 2023.

Boutland, Craig. *What Happened on D-Day?* Rosen Young Adult, 2023.

Carser, A. R. *The US Decision to Drop the Atomic Bomb.* Core Library, 2021.

Gale, Ryan. The *Manhattan Project.* Core Library, 2021.

London, Martha. *Atomic Bomb Survivor Stories.* Core Library, 2021.

Roscoe, Kelly (ed.). *Dwight D. Eisenhower.* Britannica Educational Publishing, 2016.

Websites

www.army.mil/d-day/index.html
Learn more about D-Day at the official website of the U.S. Army.

http://atomicbombmuseum.org/
The website of the Atomic Bomb Museum provides an overview of the historical events of August 1945.

www.ducksters.com/history/world_war_ii/ww2_atomic_bomb.php
This website provides Information on the building and dropping of the atomic bomb.

https://education.nationalgeographic.org/resource/date-which-will-live-infamy/)
Take a look at the historical events of December 7, 1941, when Japan attacked Pearl Harbor.

www.nps.gov/valr/index.htm
Explore the Pearl Harbor National Memorial.

https://veterans.gc.ca/en/remembrance/wars-and-conflicts/second-world-war/d-day-and-the-battle-of-normandy
Learn more about Canada's role in D-Day and listen to first-hand accounts from Canadians who were there.

INDEX

aircraft carriers 9, 16
Allies 18, 25, 26, 29, 30, 42, 43, 44, 45, 46, 50, 51, 54, 55, 56, 57, 58, 60, 61
atomic bomb 19, 22–24, 26, 27, 28, 29, 30, 31, 35, 36, 38, 39, 40, 41
Axis powers 25, 42

battleships 4, 12, 13, 14, 16, 21, 26, 35, 50
bombers 9, 11, 14, 15, 20, 31, 46, 50
Britain 7, 17, 18, 25, 27, 30, 41, 42, 44, 48, 51, 52, 55, 56, 57

Calais 45
Canada 25, 27, 42, 46, 51, 52, 58–59
Cherbourg 54
Comprehensive Test Ban Treaty 41
Cousins, Norman 41

deaths (from nuclear blast) 36–39

Einstein, Albert 24
Eisenhower, Dwight 44, 46, 47, 51
England 45, 46, 48, 50
Enola Gay 31, 32
Europe 4, 7, 18, 25, 28, 30, 42, 43, 44, 60, 61

Fat Man (bomb) 23, 34
France 7, 25, 41, 44, 47, 48, 50, 51, 54, 60

Gadget (bomb) 29
Garcia, Juan Pujol 45
Germany 7, 18, 19, 24, 25, 26, 30, 42–43, 44, 57, 60
Gold Beach 51, 52, 55, 56

hibakusha 38, 41
Hirohito 6, 35
Hiroshima 19, 22–23, 32–33, 34, 36, 37, 38, 39, 40, 41
Hitler, Adolf 25, 42–43, 45, 60, 61
Hobart, Percy 57
Hollis, Stanley 56

internment camps 19
Italy 18, 25, 42

Japan 4–7, 8, 9, 10, 11, 12, 14, 15, 16, 17, 18, 19, 20, 21, 22, 23, 25, 26, 28, 30, 31, 32, 34, 35, 40, 41, 42, 60
Japanese planes (Zeroes) 12, 14, 17, 20
Juno Beach 51, 52, 58–59

landing craft 47, 51, 52, 54–55, 58
Little Boy (bomb) 31, 32, 34

Martin, Charlie 59
memorials 12, 21, 39, 40, 61

Normandy 51, 60, 61

oil 5, 6, 7, 16, 21, 25
Omaha Beach 51–53
Operation Neptune 47, 51, 52
Operation Overlord 44, 46, 47
Oppenheimer, J. Robert 26

paratroopers 46, 48–49
Peace Memorial Park 39, 40
Philippines 17, 20
Poland 7, 25, 42
Potsdam Conference 30

radiation 36, 37, 38–39
Ray, John 49
Roosevelt, Franklin 7, 18, 19, 24, 25, 26, 28
Russell, Ken 49
Russia 25, 41, 42, 43

Sainte-Mère-Église 49
Sasaki, Sadako 39
Stalin, Joseph 30, 43
Steele, John 49
Sweeney, Charles 34
Sword Beach 51, 52, 56–57

Tanimoto, Kiyoshi 41
tanks 16, 45, 46, 51, 55, 56, 57, 58
Tibbets, Paul, Jr. 32
Trinity test 29
Truman, Harry 28, 30–31
Turner, Richmond 20

United States 4, 5, 7, 8, 10, 16, 17, 18, 19, 20, 21, 24, 25, 26, 27, 28, 30, 34, 35, 40, 41, 42, 46, 48, 49, 51, 52, 53, 54, 55
U.S. Navy 4, 7, 11, 13, 16, 35
USS *Arizona* 12, 13, 21
USS *Maryland* 14
USS *Missouri* 21, 35
USS *Nevada* 14
USS *Oklahoma* 14
USS *Ward* 9
USS *West Virginia* 12
Utah Beach 51, 52, 54

V-J Day 35

Warden, Horace 15
weapons 12, 42, 44, 46, 50, 51, 53, 55, 57

Yamamoto, Isoroku 6, 8, 18